CONTENTS

Machines at home 4

Machines in a bedroom.............................. 6

In the playroom 8

Remote-controlled cars 10

In the bathroom....................................... 12

Bathroom gadgets.................................... 14

In the kitchen... 16

Meals with microwaves 18

In the sitting room................................... 20

How a DVD player works 22

Keeping it clean....................................... 24

How vacuum cleaners work..................... 26

At home with technology 28

Glossary.. 30

Find out more 31

Index 32

Some words are printed in bold, **like this**. You can find out what they mean by looking in the glossary.

MACHINES AT HOME

Our homes are full of technology. We use **machines** in every room of the house. There are even some that we might not think of as machines!

What is a machine?

A machine does work for us. Some machines do things we cannot do alone, such as a can opener that opens tins. Other machines save us work or do a job better than us. We can wash clothes by hand, but it is hard work and washing machines clean clothes better and faster!

Here the spoon is a **lever**. Levers are rods that rest on a point called the **fulcrum**. Here the fulcrum is the edge of the tin. When you push down on the long end of the lever, the short end lifts the lid.

Powering machines

Machines need **energy** to make them work. We make some simple machines, such as scissors, work using our own energy. Other machines, such as microwave ovens, run on **electricity**.

What work do the machines in this picture do?

USING FORCES

A machine makes a **force** bigger. A force is a pushing or pulling action. Machines use forces to move parts that do work. A blender pushes blades quickly through fruit to whizz up a smoothie.

MACHINES IN A BEDROOM

Some of the things in your bedroom work because of **springs**. There are springs in a mattress. When a spring is stretched or squashed it creates a **force** in the opposite direction. This is because the spring tries to get back to its original shape. When you lie down on a bed, mattress springs push upwards against you to support your weight.

This pen works because of a spring. When the pen button is down, it squashes the spring and pushes out the pen nib. When the button is released, the spring returns to its original, longer length, and the nib moves back inside the holder.

Spring

Nib

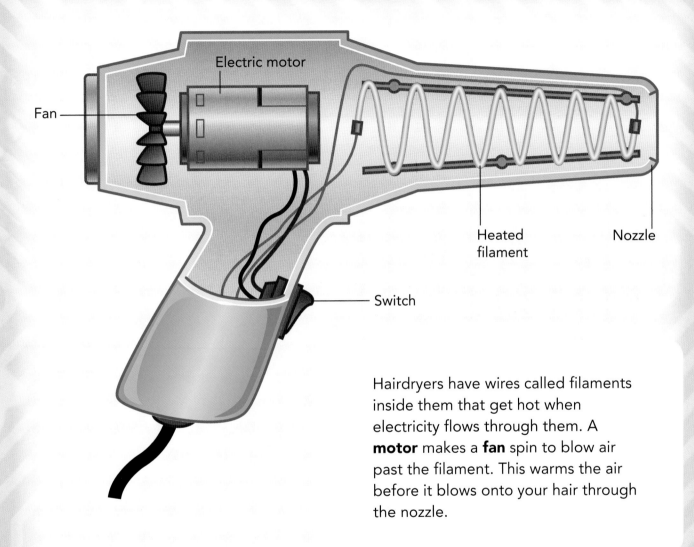

Electric motor

Fan

Heated filament

Nozzle

Switch

Hairdryers have wires called filaments inside them that get hot when electricity flows through them. A **motor** makes a **fan** spin to blow air past the filament. This warms the air before it blows onto your hair through the nozzle.

Powered by electricity

Many **machines** in the bedroom run on **electricity**. Hairdryers plug into wall sockets and run on electricity. Torches and MP3 players usually run on electrical **energy** stored in **batteries**. A battery contains special metals and chemicals that produce electricity. The electricity flows when the ends of a battery are connected to form a loop, or **circuit**.

Some of the toys in a playroom have wheels and **axles**. An axle is a rod that connects to the middle of a wheel. On a toy car, the axle turns when you make the wheels turn by pushing the car. In a real car, the **engine** turns the axle, and the axle turns the wheel.

Axle

Wheel

Wheels and axles are machines that help cars and trucks move.

IN THE FUTURE

In the future there will be more SMART toys. SMART toys have a computer chip inside them. This allows them to answer questions, obey commands, or do other clever tricks!

A yo-yo is made up of two 'wheels' connected by an axle. The axle has string wound around it. When you throw a yo-yo, the axle spins!

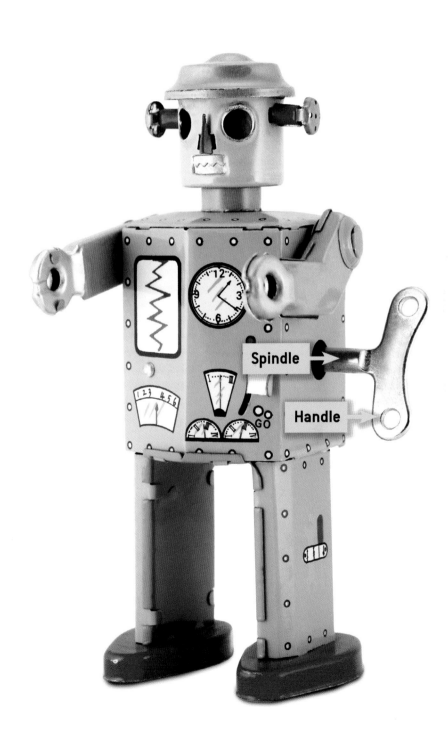

Wind-up toys

The key of a wind-up toy has a handle that acts as a wheel. The **spindle** (straight part) acts as an axle. The handle turns the spindle. The spindle is attached to a **spring**. Turning the key tightens the spring. Releasing the key lets the spring unwind, which makes the toy move.

Turning the key gives this toy the **energy** it needs to move!

Spindle

Handle

REMOTE-CONTROLLED CARS

You can make remote-controlled cars like this one go faster, slower, and turn left or right just by touching a button! This works by using **radio waves**.

Radio waves are all around us, but we do not notice. They are invisible, so we cannot see them. Radio waves are signals that carry information for televisions, radios, and mobile telephones too. A radio changes the signals to sound waves, and a television changes them into sound and light waves. It is the radio waves used in this car that make it move.

To control the car, you press the buttons on the handset. A **transmitter** inside transmits (sends) instructions to the car to make it move.

IN THE FUTURE

Most remote-controlled cars are still powered by **batteries**, but in the future many will probably use water, sunlight, or fuel cells to make them work.

This remote-controlled car is powered by a rechargeable battery pack, but some run on normal batteries.

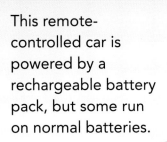

3. Inside the car there is a **receiver**. This receives signals from the transmitter and acts on those instructions. If you press the button to go right, the receiver gets this message and turns the car right.

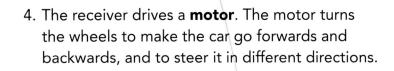

4. The receiver drives a **motor**. The motor turns the wheels to make the car go forwards and backwards, and to steer it in different directions.

2. A transmitter inside the handset is a device that sends signals to the car using radio waves.

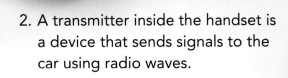

1. The handset has buttons that you use to control the car.

Some of the **machines** in the bathroom, such as taps and toilets, control the water we use to wash and to get rid of waste. Have you ever wondered how taps and toilets really work?

How taps turn on

The **spindle** of a tap has a screw-thread. This is like a tiny ramp going round and round the spindle. Screws change turning movements into up or down movements. When you turn the tap handle, it turns the spindle. The spindle lifts or lowers a washer to let water in or stop it flowing.

Tap handle

Spindle

Screw-thread

Washer

Valve

Turning a tap on lifts the washer. This lets water flow into the tap through an opening called a valve.

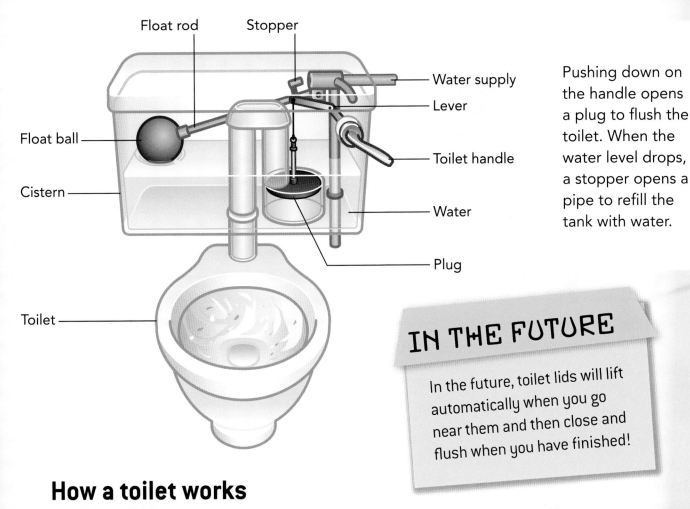

Float rod   Stopper

Water supply

Lever

Toilet handle

Water

Plug

Float ball

Cistern

Toilet

Pushing down on the handle opens a plug to flush the toilet. When the water level drops, a stopper opens a pipe to refill the tank with water.

IN THE FUTURE

In the future, toilet lids will lift automatically when you go near them and then close and flush when you have finished!

How a toilet works

Toilets flush waste away using water stored in a cistern tank.

1. When you press the handle, a **lever** pulls up a plug and water flows out of the cistern and into the toilet.

2. The falling water level in the cistern makes the float ball sink and the float rod move. This opens a stopper, or valve, at the other end and allows water to flow into the cistern.

3. As water fills the cistern again, the float ball rises. This makes the float rod push the valve closed to stop water flowing into the tank when it is full.

BATHROOM GADGETS

You can find several electric gadgets in a bathroom, such as lights, electric showers, and electric shavers. Some electric toothbrushes have brush heads that move back and forth up to 30,000 times a minute to clean our teeth!

- When you turn on the switch, an electric **circuit** is connected. This makes a **motor** inside the toothbrush start to spin.

- Just beneath the brush head there is a device that changes the fast spinning movement of the motor into a back and forth movement in the brush head.

- When you slide the toothbrush onto its holder, **electricity** flows into the toothbrush. This power is stored inside a **battery**, ready for the next time you brush.

- The outer case is made of tough plastic, and the on-off switch is covered in thin, bendy rubber. This stops water and toothpaste getting into the motor and electric parts inside. If this happened it might not work!

AT WORK

SINGING TEETH!

Scientists have invented a toothbrush that plays music while you brush your teeth. It sends sound waves through your teeth and jawbone to your ear. It plays for two minutes – the time dentists suggest we spend brushing every morning and night!

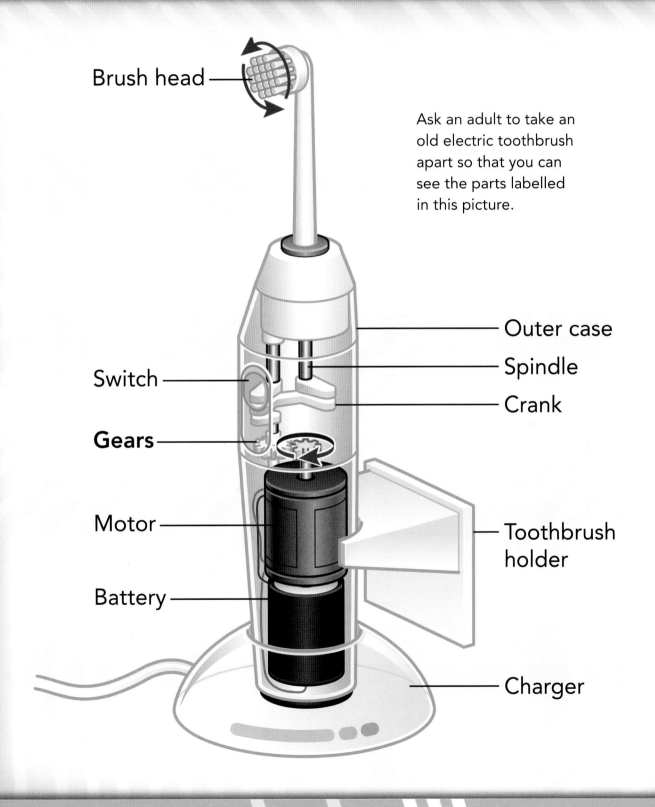

Brush head

Ask an adult to take an old electric toothbrush apart so that you can see the parts labelled in this picture.

Outer case

Spindle

Switch

Crank

Gears

Motor

Toothbrush holder

Battery

Charger

Most kitchens are filled with **machines**. Some are simple and hand-powered. Many are powered by **electricity** and work at the press of a button.

Wheels with teeth

Gears are wheels with teeth around the edge that are linked together. Gears can increase the power and change the direction of a **force**. For example, when a wheel with six teeth turns a wheel with twelve teeth, the larger wheel turns half as fast, but it turns with more force. When you twist the handle of a can opener, this moves gears that turn a metal wheel. The metal wheel cuts down into the tin.

Can openers are machines that make it simple to cut through metal.

Gears

Feel the heat

Toasters work by changing electrical **energy** into heat energy. When electricity flows through special wires inside a toaster, it makes the wires heat up and glow red. The hot wires cook bread and make toast.

How does this machine cook and pop your toast?

AT WORK

WHAT MAKES TOAST POP UP?

When you press a handle to lower bread into a toaster, it pushes the bread holder down on **springs**. When the timer turns the toaster off automatically, the spring-loaded tray is released and the toast pops out!

MEALS WITH MICROWAVES

What's cooking in the kitchen? Many **machines** in the kitchen use heat **energy** to cook food. For example, food cooks in a grill by absorbing heat rays. Like heat, microwaves are an invisible kind of energy that can travel through the air.

Microwave magic

How do microwave ovens cook food so quickly? Everything on Earth, including food, is made up of millions of particles (tiny pieces so small we cannot see them). When something is hot, the particles inside it are moving about. Microwaves can make the particles inside food move very quickly, and this is how they cook the food fast.

AT WORK

MELTING MOMENTS!

A scientist discovered the idea of microwave ovens by accident. He was working on some other equipment when he noticed that microwaves from it were melting a bar of chocolate in his pocket!

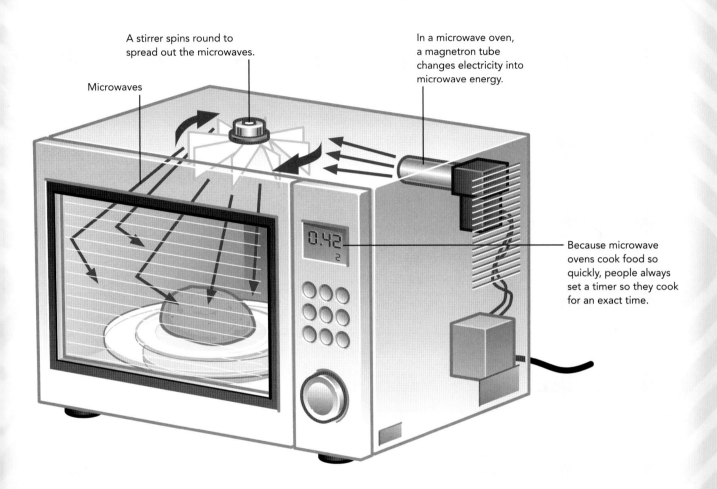

A stirrer spins round to spread out the microwaves.

Microwaves

In a microwave oven, a magnetron tube changes electricity into microwave energy.

Because microwave ovens cook food so quickly, people always set a timer so they cook for an exact time.

Microwave ovens are very efficient because they cook for a short time so use less **electricity** than other kinds of ovens to cook the same amount of food.

IN THE SITTING ROOM

Many of the **machines** in the sitting room entertain us. We listen to music on CD players, watch programmes on TV, play games on a games console, or chat on the telephone.

Speaking and listening

When you speak into a telephone, a **microphone** collects the sounds of your voice. A microphone turns these sounds into electrical signals. The signals travel to another phone. The person you are calling hears your voice because a **speaker** inside their phone turns the signals back into sounds.

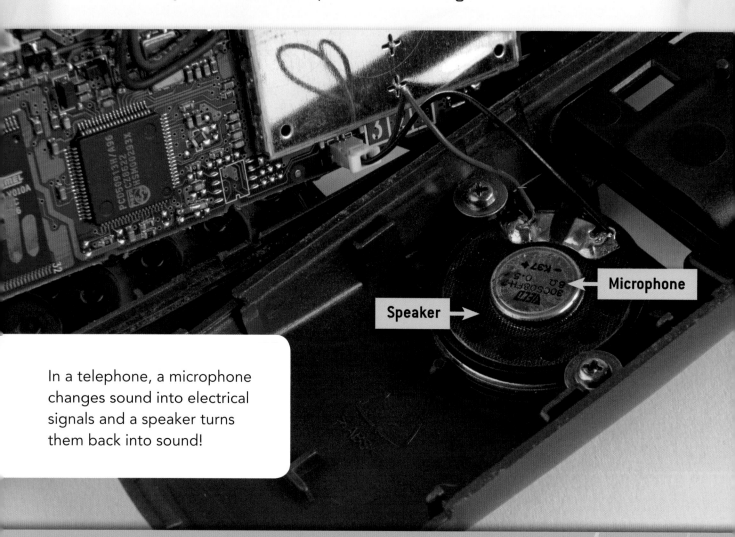

Microphone

Speaker

In a telephone, a microphone changes sound into electrical signals and a speaker turns them back into sound!

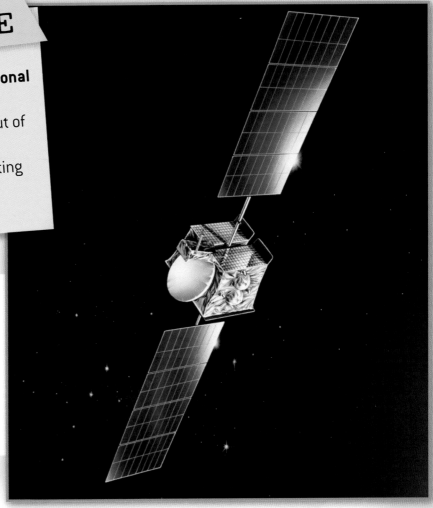

IN THE FUTURE

In the future, **three-dimensional** (3D) televisions will show images that seem to leap out of the screens at us! Some companies are already testing 3D TVs in their workshops.

It is amazing to think that the signals bringing images to your TV screen may have bounced off satellites in space like this one!

Signals from space!

How do televisions bring us pictures and sounds from the other side of the world? First a programme is recorded by a camera and sent in the form of invisible signals to a **satellite** in space. The satellite bounces the signals back to different places on Earth. A satellite dish collects the signals and passes them to a **receiver**. The receiver changes the signals into sound and pictures on the television set.

HOW A DVD PLAYER WORKS

DVD players are digital **machines**. In digital machines, sounds and images are changed into signals that represent a series of zeros and ones. This is how information is stored on computers. DVD players work using **lasers**. Lasers make special beams of light that help to turn the signals back into sounds and pictures for us to enjoy!

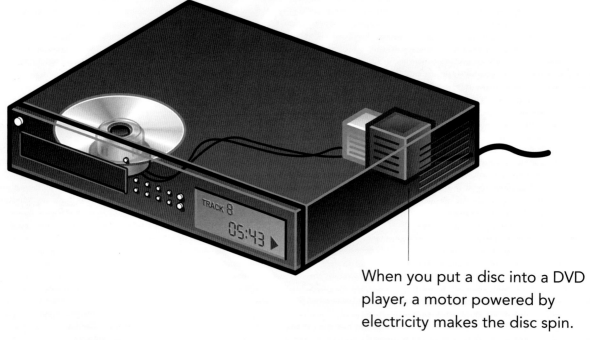

When you put a disc into a DVD player, a motor powered by electricity makes the disc spin.

AT WORK

CD OR DVD?

CDs and DVDs work in the same way. The difference is that a DVD can hold much more digital information than a CD. That is why a DVD can store images, sounds, and music, as well as games and other information.

When the laser beam sees a dip, it produces the number 1. When the surface is flat the laser registers a 0.

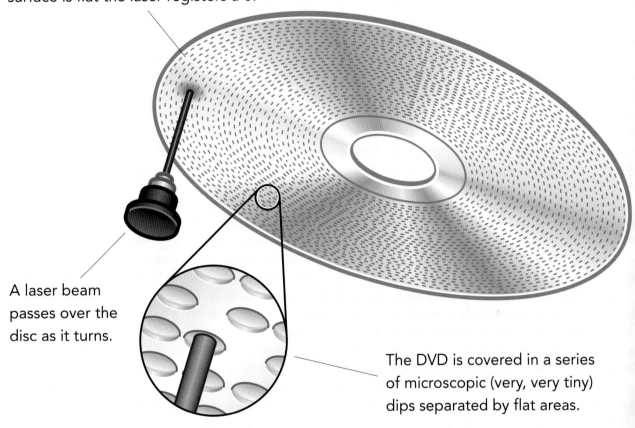

A laser beam passes over the disc as it turns.

The DVD is covered in a series of microscopic (very, very tiny) dips separated by flat areas.

A laser inside a DVD player collects digital information. Then the DVD player quickly changes this sequence of 0s and 1s back into an electric signal, and then back into sounds and images to play your film.

KEEPING IT CLEAN

Cleaning might not be much fun, but imagine how much harder it would be without technology like washing **machines**, dishwashers, and vacuum cleaners!

Washing the dishes

Inside a dishwasher is a **motor**. The motor pumps water into several sprayers. These spray hot water and soap onto dirty dishes. The dirty water then drains away and clean water is sprayed onto dishes to rinse them. Finally a heater or hot-air **fan** dries the dishes.

Would you rather wash dishes by hand or let a dishwasher do the work?

In a spin

A motor turns the drum inside a washing machine. The clothes inside the drum are tumbled in soapy water and then in clean water. To get rid of the water the drum spins very fast. This pushes the clothes and the water against the sides of the drum. The water flows out through holes in the drum, which leaves the clothes drier.

Controls operate a small computer that tells the washing machine how long to wash and spin.

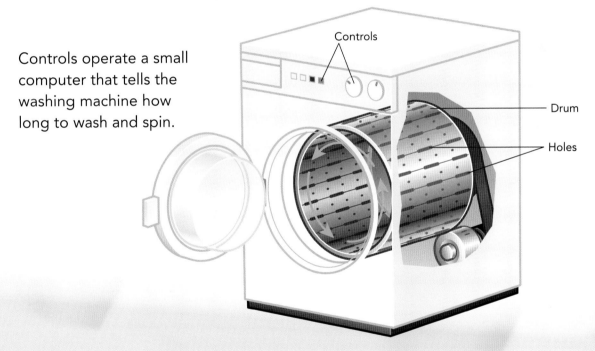

Controls

Drum

Holes

AT WORK

THE SPINNING FORCE

When things move very quickly in a circle they are affected by centripetal **force**. This force keeps objects spinning in a circle.

HOW VACUUM CLEANERS WORK

Why is using a vacuum cleaner like drinking through a straw? They both work by sucking up air. Vacuum means 'empty of air'. You create a vacuum in a straw when you suck the air out of it. This causes the drink in the glass to come up the straw to fill the empty space. Vacuum cleaners use vacuum suction to remove dirt from carpets.

You suck through a straw to create a flow of liquid into your mouth. Vacuum cleaners use suction to create a flow or movement of air.

Follow steps 1 to 6 to find out how a vacuum cleaner works!

6. In this machine the filter is a bag that can be removed and thrown away. Some vacuum cleaner filters trap dirt in a tank that can be removed and emptied.

5. The dirt-filled air is sucked through a filter. A filter is a material with lots of tiny holes. Air passes through the holes and out of the **machine**. Dirt is trapped in the filter.

3. The spinning fan creates a flowing stream of air up through the vacuum cleaner that creates suction.

1. A **motor** turns a **fan**.

4. The strong suction carries dirt inside the vacuum cleaner with the air.

2. The motor also turns a brush to dislodge dirt on the floor.

AT WORK

ROBOT CLEANERS

Robot vacuum cleaners are small enough to go under furniture. **Sensors** stop them bumping into things, and they turn themselves off when the programmed length of time is over.

AT HOME WITH TECHNOLOGY

There are lots of **machines** in the home, but many of them work using similar technology.

SPRINGS

When a **spring** is stretched or squashed, it creates a **force** in the opposite direction because the spring tries to get back to its original shape. When the spring is released it moves back to its original shape. This movement can be used in machines such as:

- Mattresses – to cushion a body on a bed.

- Pens – to push out and return a nib in a pen.

- Toasters – to pop-up your toast when it is cooked.

LEVERS

A **lever** is a rod that rests on a point called a **fulcrum**.

- A pair of scissors is a simple machine made of two metal levers.

- The handle on a toilet is a lever that lifts a plug inside the cistern tank.

- A can opener handle is like a lever that pushes the cutting blade into the top of a tin.

ELECTRIC MOTORS

An electric **motor** is a machine that uses electrical **energy** to make machine parts move. Motors are used in the following machines:

- Hairdryer – a motor turns the **fan** that blows hot air.

- Remote-controlled car – a motor turns the wheels.

- Electric toothbrush – a motor spins the toothbrush head.

- Vacuum cleaner – a motor turns a fan to create suction.

- Washing machine – a motor turns a drum to tumble the clothes about.

- Microwave oven – a motor turns the food tray so food cooks evenly.

ELECTRO-MAGNETIC ENERGY

- Electro-magnetic energy includes forms of energy such as **radio waves**, microwaves, and light rays.

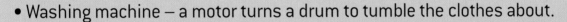

- Televisions, remote-controlled cars, and radios all receive radio waves and change the signals into sound, pictures, and movement.

- DVD and CD players both create signals from discs using **lasers**. This information is converted into sounds and images.

- Microwave ovens use microwave energy to cook food.

GLOSSARY

axle rod that connects to the centre of a wheel. Axles and wheels are parts that allow vehicles to move.

battery container of chemicals that produces electricity when properly connected in a circuit

circuit loops or circular pathways through which electricity flows. When we flick a switch a circuit is completed so electricity can flow and turn a machine on.

electricity type of energy we use as a source of power to make machines work. TVs and computers are powered by electricity.

energy force that makes things work. Some machines are powered by electrical energy.

engine machine that uses fuel to create movement in machines

fan device for creating a current of air

force pushing or pulling action. We use a pushing force to make wheelbarrows move.

fulcrum the support or point on which a lever rests. The fulcrum on a seesaw is always in the middle of the plank (lever).

gear wheel with teeth around the edge. One gear wheel turns another because the teeth interlock with each other.

laser narrow, intense beam of light energy. Laser beams are used to read CDs and DVDs.

lever simple machine that helps us lift loads. A seesaw is a kind of lever.

machine device that helps us do work. Hammers are machines that help us bang nails into wood.

microphone device that changes sounds into electric signals. A microphone in a telephone handset changes our voices into signals.

motor machine that converts, or changes, electrical energy into rotating or turning energy

radio waves invisible rays of energy that travel through air. Radio waves carry information for televisions, radios and mobile telephones.

receiver device that receives radio or television signals. Receivers convert electrical signals into sounds, images or signals to create movement.

satellite device in space. Satellites circle Earth receiving and transmitting signals.

sensor device that senses light or other signals and produces an electronic signal from them. Some light sensors tell when it is dark and turn lights on.

speaker device that converts electrical signals into sounds. Telephones, televisions, and radios contain speakers.

spindle rod or bar that can spin. When you turn a tap, the spindle turns too.

spring coil of metal. When you squash a spring, it creates a force that is released when the spring goes back to its original shape.

three-dimensional something with height, width, and depth

transmitter device that sends out radio, television, or telephone signals. Remote control sets contain transmitters.

FIND OUT MORE

Books

Flick a Switch: How Electricity Gets to Your Home, Barbara Seuling (Holiday House, 2003)

In the Home (How Things Have Changed), Jon Richards (Chrysalis Education, 2005)

Inventions We Use at Home (Everyday Inventions), Jane Bidder (Gareth Stevens Publishing, 2006)

Switched On, Flushed Down, Tossed Out: Investigating the Hidden Workings of Your Home, Trudee Romanek (Annick Press, 2005)

The Science of Forces: Projects with Experiments on Forces and Machines (Tabletop Scientist), Steve Parker (Heinemann Library, 2005)

Websites

http://teacher.scholastic.com/dirtrep/simple/index.htm
Look at this website to investigate simple machines.

http://pbskids.org/wayback/tech1900/index.html
Find out about machines invented in the past, such as early telephones.

www.explainthatstuff.com
Type in a machine, such as washing machine or electric toothbrush, and find out more about how it works.

www.edheads.org/activities/simple-machines/
On this website you can learn more about simple machines such as levers. You can also play games.

INDEX

axles 8, 9

bathrooms 12-15
batteries 7, 11, 14, 15
blenders 5

can openers 4, 16, 28
CDs/CD players 22, 29
circuits 7, 14
cisterns 13
computer chips 8

digital machines 22-23
dishwashers 24
DVD players 22-23, 29

electric motors 7, 11, 14, 15,
    24, 25, 27, 29
electric toothbrushes 14-15, 29
electrical signals 20
electricity 5, 7, 14, 16, 17, 19, 29
electro-magnetic energy 29
energy 5, 7, 9, 17, 18, 29
    electro-magnetic 29
engines 8

fans 7, 24, 27, 29
filters 27
float ball 13
force 5, 6, 16, 28
    centripetal 25
fulcrum 4, 28

gears 16

hairdryers 7, 29

kitchens 16-19

lasers 22, 23
levers 4, 13, 28

machines 4, 5, 7, 12, 16, 18,
    20, 22, 28-29
mattresses 6, 28
microphones 20
microwaves 5, 18-19, 29
MP3 players 7

pens 6, 28
pushing and pulling 5

radio waves 10, 11, 29
receivers 11, 21
remote-controlled cars 10-11,
    29

satellites 21
scissors 5, 28
screws 12
sensors 27
sitting rooms 20-3
speakers 20
spindles 9, 12
spoons 4
springs 6, 9, 17, 28

taps 12
telephones 10, 20
televisions 10, 21, 29
    three-dimensional
    televisions 21
toasters 17, 28
toilets 13, 28

torches 7
toys 8-11
    remote-controlled cars
        10-11, 29
    SMART toys 8
    wind-up toys 9
transmitters 10, 11

vacuum cleaners 26-27, 29
    robot cleaners 27
valves 12, 13

washers 12
washing machines 4, 25, 29
wheels 8, 16

yo-yos 8